EXPLORING
Historic Upcountry

EXPLORING
Historic Upcountry

Jill Engledow

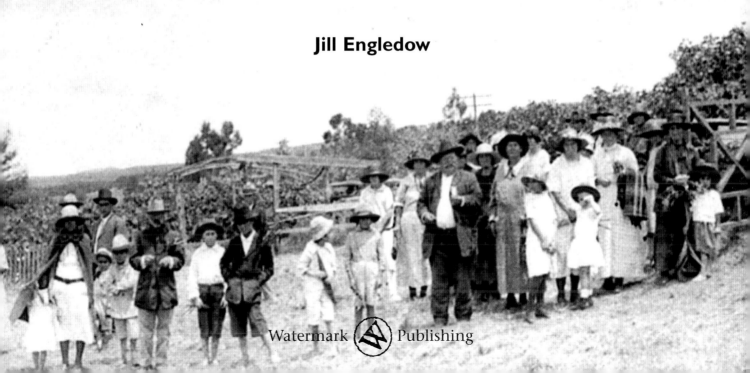

Watermark W Publishing

Design by
Gonzalez Design Co.

Production by
Randall Chun Design

Library of Congress Catalog Number: 2001097741
ISBN 0-9705787-5-X

Exploring Historic Upcountry is an ongoing
community effort. Readers with additional
information about any of the photos or captions
 in this book are invited to contact the publisher
at the mailing address or e-mail address below.

Watermark Publishing
1000 Bishop Street, Suite 501-A
Honolulu, HI 96813
Telephone: Toll-free 1-866-900-BOOK
Web site: www.bookshawaii.net
e-mail: sales@watermark.net

Printed in China

Contents

1 **Foreword**

2 **Introduction**

4 **Chapter One**
Pā'ia

40 **Chapter Two**
Hāmākuapoko,
Pa'uwela and Ha'ikū

52 **Chapter Three**
Makawao

82 **Chapter Four**
Hāli'imaile and Keāhua

90 **Chapter Five**
Kula

100 **Chapter Six**
Kēōkea and 'Ulupalakua

121 **Resources**

122 **Index**

123 **Upcountry Map**

Acknowledgments

Many people contributed to this history of Upcountry Maui, sharing not only photographs but introductions, suggestions and memories. I am always amazed and grateful at the generosity and trust shown by those who are willing to lend their precious old photographs so that they may be enjoyed by others who love Maui. Many thanks to Gail Ainsworth of Maui Community College; Beryl Bal, Gail Burns and Roslyn Lightfoot of the Maui Historical Society; Gaylord Kubota of the Alexander & Baldwin Sugar Museum; Jean Fiddes, Janet Makua and the Rev. Heather Mueller-Fitch of St. John's Episcopal Church; Peter Baldwin and Camille Lyons of Haleakala Ranch; Wendy Rice Peterson and Henry Rice of Kaonoulu Ranch; C. Pardee Erdman and Donna Waters of 'Ulupalakua Ranch, and Irvin Yamada of Photography by Irvin. Thanks also to Leona Balthazar, Virgie Cantorna, David Cup Choy, Alan DeCoite, Shirley DePonte of Holy Ghost Church, Kay Fukumoto, Albert and Amy Watanabe, Jim Fuller, Cliff and Pauline Green, A.K. Hew, Janie Karimoto and the Rev. Ronald Kobata of Makawao Hongwanji, Nobu Kitada, Victor Kobayashi, Cindy Lawrence, Rhonda Lincoln, Terry Lock, Eunice Garcia and Doug MacCluer of Maui Land & Pineapple Co., Terry and Allan Marciel, Warren McCord, Domingo Molina, David Morihara, Judge Boyd Mossman, Ruth Mukai, Laurel Murphy, Charlotte Nakamura, Lynn Nakamura-Tengan, Stephanie Ohigashi, Jeff Reiss, Ernest and Alene Rezents, Steve Rose, Mary Cameron Sanford, Betty Komoda Shibuya, Dan Shigeta, Stephanie Sheppard, Jay Slaughter of Makawao Union Church, Clara Sodetani, Jimmy Tam Sing, Wayne Tanaka, Bill Tavares, Charlene Thompson, Randy von Tempsky and Emily Young.

vi

Foreword

On Maui, "Upcountry" covers a broad area of forest, farmland and meadows stretching across the slopes of Haleakalā. Upcountry's unique natural beauty—jacaranda and eucalyptus trees, open pasture, vegetable and flower farms—is complemented by a growing residential community and a century-old ranching tradition. Those of us who've grown up here and make Upcountry our home wouldn't trade if for anywhere else in the world.

Upcountry Maui is a special world of rodeos and polo ponies; Kula onions and cabbages; carnations and protea blossoms; and breezy days and cool, starlit nights. Recent years have brought new homes and remodeling projects to the area, as more and more people discover this unique corner of the Hawaiian Islands. That makes *Exploring Historic Upcountry* all the more useful as a hands-on guide to the area's rich history.

My life has been dedicated to the enjoyment and preservation of Upcountry's ranch culture. When we were kids, my friends and I thought nothing of saddling up and riding for miles just to hang out together—galloping up and down the dirt roads and generally terrorizing the neighborhood. Today, we've introduced the Holiday Festival and Parade, an annual December event in the town of Makawao celebrating the *paniolo*—the Hawaiian cowboy. Also on the drawing board is a Paniolo Museum for the town of Makawao, famous for a half-century as the home of the July 4th Rodeo and Parade—Hawai'i's biggest and best rodeo. As the 50th State's "Cowboy Town," Makawao is a natural home for a museum that will be of great interest to both Maui visitors and residents.

For now, you can wander through the pages of *Exploring Historic Upcountry*—and discover the special feeling enjoyed by those of us lucky enough to call Upcountry home.

Aloha,

Peter Baldwin
Fourth Generation Rancher
Haleakala Ranch

Introduction

The story of Upcountry Maui is a story of the land and the people who work it. From the Hawaiians of old—who planted sweet potatoes and harvested sandalwood—to the farmers of today with their onions and protea, growing things have provided a livelihood in this broad area that Maui people call simply "Upcountry."

The other defining quality of this lush region hugging the slopes of Haleakala is sheer natural beauty. Much of the land is still in pasture—vast green fields rolling up the flanks of the great volcano. From 'Ulupalakua, Kula, Pukalani and many places in Makawao and Ha'ikū, there are fine views of lowlands, ocean and the West Maui Mountains.

Once, the highlands were forested with scented sandalwood. After the Western world discovered the Hawaiian Islands, however, ships' captains enticed the *ali'i* (chiefs) into trade for consumer goods, and the mountainsides were stripped of their original forests. In later years, ranchers reforested the area with imported trees. The lands of Haleakala Ranch, in particular, became known for the fragrant but foreign eucalyptus. Springtime is now especially wondrous in Kula, as the jacaranda scatter their lavender blossoms and wattle trees flower in gold.

Upcountry's soil and climate have always attracted farmers. In Kula, Chinese immigrants grew potatoes that sustained hungry whalers and California gold seekers. Ranchers fattened their cattle in emerald pastures, and Hawaiian *paniolo* (cowboys) cared for them with skills that rivaled those of the best cowboys in the American West. Japanese farmers raised vegetables so precious to the military during World War II that local buyers were priced out of the market.

From Pūlehu to Ha'ikū, an industry grew from the early efforts of Henry P. Baldwin and Samuel Alexander, missionaries' sons who began in 1870 with 12 acres of sugar cane on the hillside below Makawao. The people who worked the smaller plantations that eventually combined into Maui Agricultural Co.—and later Hawaiian Commercial & Sugar Co.—lived in "camps," small close-knit neighborhoods scattered across the northwestern slope of Haleakalā.

The Baldwin family did not limit their enterprises to sugar. Henry P. Baldwin was one of the partners who in 1888 purchased the land that would become Haleakala Ranch. By 1925 the ranch was entirely owned by Baldwin family members. For a time,

'Ulupalakua Ranch was also owned by Baldwins, while Kaonoulu Ranch is today owned by the Rice family, descendants of a daughter of H.P. Baldwin. It was Henry's brother, David Dwight Baldwin, who first planted pineapple at Haʻikū in 1890, and a Baldwin son-in-law, J. Walter Cameron, who headed up the merger of the various pineapple companies that became Maui Land & Pineapple Co.

Elsewhere Upcountry, Rev. Jonathan S. Green founded Protestant churches and promoted the growing of wheat in Makawao, a product successfully marketed to California gold miners. Sugar planter Tong Akana and rancher Sun Mei were among the most successful of the Chinese immigrants, who at one time were the dominant population in Kula. And Father James Beissel built Catholic churches across the large Upcountry district to serve the Portuguese population. Some immigrants labored in plantation fields their whole lives, while others finished their contracts and struck out on their own. The communities of Kula, Makawao, Haʻikū and Pāʻia all saw the growth of small businesses run by entrepreneurs out of the plantations.

The turmoil of World War II disturbed Maui's rural tranquility. Military troops trained in the jungles and on the beaches and spent their leave time in the island's little towns. Young men went off to war and returned with a new outlook. No longer content to work in the fields, they used their GI Bill benefits to educate themselves to lead postwar Hawaiʻi. With the residential development of the town of Kahului, some of the old camps simply disappeared, covered over by sugar cane.

After Hawaiʻi statehood, Upcountry's growth slowed considerably. The action now was on Maui's leeward shores, where pristine beaches provided the raw material for glamorous new resorts. Only with the islandwide population growth of the 1970s did Upcountry begin attracting new residents again, bringing life to the little towns that had slumbered for so many years. Pastures filled with new homes, and Upcountry became a sought-after bedroom community.

The photographs in this collection give a glimpse of the changing face of Upcountry, over time and over the wide area broadly described by that term. Some of the places pictured now exist only in memory, while others look just as they did decades ago. Each of the photos is keyed to the gatefold map at the back of the book. Those who follow the map past the storefronts of Pāʻia and Makawao, or through the pastures of Haʻikū and Haleakala, will find the essential beauty of this fertile district just as striking as it has been during Upcountry's rich, colorful history.

Upper Pā'ia, 1957

Upper Pā'ia ceased to exist not long after this photo was taken. Today fields of sugar cane blow in the breeze that once cooled the homes and stores shown here. Above the mill are Paia Store, a baseball field, Paia Hongwanji and villages such as Skill Camp, Store Camp, Nashiwa Camp and Spanish Camp. Former residents of Upper Pā'ia often are able to find their old homes on a wall-sized version of this photo that hangs in the Alexander & Baldwin Sugar Museum in the town of Pu'unene, near Kahului.

Alexander & Baldwin Sugar Museum

4

CHAPTER ONE
Pāʻia

A Changing Pāʻia

The little town of Pāʻia today consists of a few blocks of shops and restaurants near the shoreline. In the early 1900s life in Pāʻia was clearly divided between Upper Pāʻia and Lower Pāʻia. Upper Pāʻia was plantation-owned. Several camps (plantation villages) housed thousands of residents. The mill was the center of life.

Supporting the mill and its workers were establishments like the Pāʻia train depot and the Paia Store. Children walked to Paʻia School, or caught the train to Maui High School in Hāmākuapoko. There were many opportunities for recreation—from barefoot football to fishing, sumo wrestling, boxing or even playing golf on a nine-hole course near the Holy Rosary Church.

Down the hill, in Lower Pāʻia, land was privately owned around the crossroads of what is now Hāna Highway and Baldwin Avenue. The original population of Hawaiians was augmented with Chinese in the early decades of the 19th Century. When the Chinese began to move to Oʻahu about 1920, they were replaced by Japanese and other ethnic groups who were leaving the plantations.

In the years before World War II, Pāʻia flourished, with a population of about 10,000 people. Business boomed during the war, as more than 200,000 military personnel passed through Maui. But Pāʻia began to fade in the postwar years, when the plantation shut down the camps and many workers moved to the new "Dream City" subdivisions in Kahului. By 1970 the population of Pāʻia was little more than 1,500, and the camps of Upper Pāʻia were planted with sugar cane.

When the newcomers known as hippies arrived in the late '60s, Pāʻia was a sleepy, shabby town in need of paint. The first hippie store opened at 89 Hāna Highway in 1968, selling items such as handmade clothing and Da-Glo posters. Old-timers were dismayed by the hippie lifestyle, and with a tiny inventory and few customers, this Paia General Store lasted only a few months. Still, it was the beginning of new life for the town as more newcomers arrived to set up shop in old buildings.

In the 1980s Pāʻia drew an international crowd who came to windsurf at nearby Hoʻokipa Beach. The town has since become a busy tourist mecca, with boutiques and galleries joining the last few mom-and-pop stores of old Pāʻia.

5, 6, 7, 8, 9* **Merchants of Pā'ia**
Some of the landmark buildings in this 1940s photo were, from left, Paia Mercantile, the little restaurant known as Wimpy's Corner, Wong Store, Dang Dry Goods Store (with a balcony) and Matsui Restaurant. At far right, Nagata Store had opened in 1935. All the other stores have since changed owners and specialties, some of them many times. But Nagata Store is still going strong, one of only three of the old-time businesses still operating in Lower Pā'ia.
Maui Historical Society
*See map on page 123

4 **Lower Paia Theatre**

Lily Hisae Morimoto, who would later become the wife of County Chairman Eddie Tam, is shown with a man described as "a showman from Japan" outside the Lower Pa'ia Theatre. Also known as the Narumaru Theater, the Lower Paia featured Japanese films. It was one of three theaters in town during the 1930s. A second, the Princess Theater, was two blocks down the street, while the plantation-owned Paia Theater was in Upper Pa'ia. The Princess later closed, and a "New Princess" theater opened on Baldwin Avenue in 1940. *Stephanie Ohigashi Collection*

4 **Lower Paia Theatre**
One of the buildings damaged by the devastating tsunami of 1946 was the Lower Paia Theatre. The theater was on a site at the Kahului end of town now occupied by a parking lot. Lower Pā'ia, *The Maui News* reported, "took on the appearance of a war-blasted town in Normandy! Shattered stores lined the Hana Highway! Light and phone wires were down! Two residence buildings straddled the street entering the town from Kahului!" *Maui Historical Society*

4 **The Tsunami of '46**

Pā'ia town was one of the areas of Maui that was hit hardest by the tsunami caused by an undersea earthquake off the Aleutian Islands. Waves smashed into the little town on April 1, and even those who heard that something was wrong thought the warnings were an April Fool's Day joke. Once the waves arrived, residents fled for higher ground, fearing that more were on the way. Despite the tragedy, there were lighter moments—some people helped themselves to the fish found flopping on the highway when the water subsided. *Jim Fuller Collection*

3 **Hew Store**

The former Hew Store was severely damaged by the 1946 tsunami. The building, which had earlier housed a store and restaurant belonging to Sing Cha Hew, was the Hew family residence at the time the destructive waves washed ashore. The family fled and returned later to find a huge boulder downstairs. Pā'ia's only tsunami fatality, an elderly bedridden man, lived nearby. The building was repaired and became the Touchstone Gallery in the 1970s. Since 1982 it has housed the Maui Crafts Guild. *Maui Historical Society*

"Pā'ia is burning"

In the middle of a July night in 1930, Bill Tavares' father woke the boy and his brother Carl. "He said, 'Boys, Pā'ia is burning' with great sadness in his voice," Bill Tavares recalls. "I was just nine on that terrible night."

Antone F. Tavares and his two sons drove into Pā'ia, where the fire was still smoldering and smoking. Antone owned a good portion of the land on the Wailuku side of town, including Kubo's Service Station, where the fire had been stopped, perhaps by an explosion which looked to young Bill like "a balloon of fire."

When the Tavares family arrived, "some men were on top of the Pa'ia Mercantile building," Bill Tavares recounts. "They were putting water on burlap bags to save it. Miraculously, the flames did not leap across to that building. There was no fire protection, just a couple plantation trucks. There were no fire hydrants."

The fire, which for a time threatened to wipe out the entire section of Lower Pā'ia, started about 1 a.m. in a store belonging to Tam Ho at the corner of what is now Baldwin Avenue and Hāna Highway.

By 5 a.m. the fire had ruthlessly claimed some 15 stores and a number of smaller structures, *The Maui News* reported. The damages were estimated at $150,000, and about 150 persons were left homeless.

Melted plumbing connections in the buildings lowered the water pressure so much as to render firefighters helpless. "We just had to sit and watch it burn," was the way Deputy Sheriff Frank Silva described it to a reporter. When the fire jumped across the street, Silva and his men tried dynamite, but after blowing up one building abandoned the plan as futile.

Finally a pump belonging to Maui Agricultural Co. was brought into action. It pumped water from the ocean onto the charred and smoldering remains of what was once the business heart of Lower Pā'ia. This prevented the wind from picking up embers and scattering them among the undamaged buildings.

It was too late to save nearly a block of buildings owned by Antone Tavares, a rancher, businessman and politician. "He lost thousands of dollars worth of property in that fire," says Bill Tavares.

10 Pā'ia Fire

The fire of 1930 left most of this block in ashes. Arson was suspected in the blaze, which broke out early on a Sunday morning in the new store building of Tam Ho at Pā'ia's main intersection. Though hundreds of volunteers from the Upcountry district rushed to help the firefighters, insufficient water pressure allowed the flames to destroy frame structures in the immediate vicinity before jumping across the highway. Many stores and homes were completely wiped out, as was Pā'ia's police station. *Maui Historical Society*

11 **Liberty Cafe**

For many years before World War II, the Liberty Cafe *(left of telephone pole)* was a popular restaurant serving American food. A complete dinner with a steak cut to order could be had for $1.25. People came from as far away as the county seat of Wailuku to dine here, and it was a favorite of the Marines stationed at nearby Camp Maui. The cafe, later operated as Kihata's and Larry's, sat empty by the end of the 1990s. Paia Mercantile is at right, on the corner of Pā'ia Road, dubbed "Baldwin Avenue" by the military during the war. *Maui Historical Society*

12 **Paia Mercantile**

Of all the independently owned stores in Lower Pā'ia, only Paia Mercantile rivaled the plantation-operated Paia Store in size and variety of goods. The store was stockholder-owned and managed in the 1920s by chief stockholder T. Hanzawa. About a dozen employees lived behind the store, each earning a dollar a day. The store tried to fill many needs to keep its customers loyal. It remained in business until the 1970s and was later subdivided into various retail spaces.

Maui Historical Society

15 **Paia Mantokuji Mission** The Rev. Sokyo Ueoka moved to Lower Pā'ia in 1906 and established the Paia Mantokuji, then known as the Bachozan Mantokuji. He is shown here in 1946 with his wife, Tomyo, outside the present Mantokuji Mission, which was built on land the congregation acquired in 1919. The Rev. Sokyo Ueoka was succeeded by his son, Sokan, and grandson, Shuko. The succession of Ueoka ministers ended when the Rev. Shuko Ueoka died in 1990.

Clara Sodetani Collection

15 Paia Mantokuji Mission
The *bonsho* (bell) in the *shoro* (belfry) at the Mantokuji Mission on Pā'ia's shoreline was cast in 1910 as a memorial for the Sino-Japanese and Russo-Japanese wars. The names and prayers of the bell's Japanese donors are inscribed on it. The temple next to the *shoro*, built in 1921, remains standing today, despite being battered by the 1946 tsunami. The bell is still rung each evening and at New Year's celebrations and *bon* dances.
Maui Historical Society

2 **Tavares Bay**
Antone F. Tavares built this residence on the coastline between Pāʻia and Hāmākuapoko in 1914 to house his family of 12 children. The manager of the Haiku Fruit & Packing Co. in the 1920s, Tavares was also an entrepreneur and served in the Territorial Legislature from 1912 to 1930. Today, this stretch of coastline in Kūʻau is densely packed with homes. This house no longer exists, but Antone Tavares' son William and other family members live in a compound on the property overlooking what is still known as Tavares Bay. *William Tavares Collection*

| **Maui Country Club**
Tournament chairman Dr. Seiya Ohata, visiting golf pro Jimmy Ukauka and Maui Golf Association president Eddie Tam stand by the bar at the Maui Country Club after the second Maui Open Golf Championship, held in 1958. The nine-hole course opened in 1925. The Country Club is open for public play on Mondays, and the interior of its bar is still decorated with the bamboo paneling.
Stephanie Ohigashi Collection

Enterprise in Lower Pāʻia

The early shop owners of Lower Pāʻia were hard-working entrepreneurs who managed to compete with the much larger plantation-subsidized Paia Store.

Early in the century, Pāʻia storekeepers sold rice, taro and poi raised in the hamlet of Keʻanae and vegetables from Kula and surrounding plantation camps. They used coconut from Hāna to make pies. Kula farmers would drive horse-drawn wagons down to deliver their produce, spend the night and then drive home the next day with purchases from the store.

Pāʻia's entrepreneurs were an early-rising and creative lot. At Hew's Restaurant, on the mauka side of Hāna Highway, the family rose before dawn to prepare homemade noodles for their famous saimin. Satoki Ikeda risked ruining sample clothing he nailed up in the store windows as advertisements, betting correctly that this method of drawing customers would pay off in the long run. The Nashiwa family introduced their rice-loving Japanese customers to the wonders of bread, then invented recipes that would require them to use a lot of it.

One businessman who was particularly successful was Nobuichi Kobayashi. Born in Pāʻia in 1896, "Kobe" was the son of Japanese immigrants who left the plantation when their two-year contract expired. The family ran a small inn and raised horses at a time when Pāʻia was a rest stop for people riding horseback to Hāna.

As a young man, Kobe went to Honolulu to learn about auto repair, then returned to Pāʻia in 1914 and started his own auto repair and parts business. In the 1930s, he ran three times for the Board of Supervisors. His ad in *The Maui News* combined English and Hawaiian, using the nickname Kauka Otomobilia—automobile doctor.

Kobayashi was unsuccessful in his bids for office, but his businesses continue to grow. He helped to organize both Haleakala Motors and Maui Finance Co. In 1940, he opened a Pepsi-Cola and Nehi soda bottling company at the back of his Princess Theater, across the highway from N. Kobayashi Auto Supply.

Kobayashi's son, Victor, believes that his father would have been "the richest person on Maui" had he used modern business methods. Instead, "he was old-fashioned, believing that all it took was honest hard work—the physical type—to be of value to himself and his family and society."

14 **Lower Pā'ia USO**

Originally the Princess Theater owned by Nobuichi Kobayashi, this building became a USO during World War II, and then a place for servicemen on leave to stay near the end of the war. Kobayashi established the American Soda & Ice Works at the back of the building in 1940. Its present incarnation began in 1970, when Jim Fuller moved his Charley's Juice Stand there from Lahaina. It is now Charley's Restaurant and the Charley P Woofer Saloon.
Jim Fuller Collection

21

13 Pā'ia Auto Pioneers
Nobuichi Kobayashi, age 15, plays chauffeur for his father, Kyutaro, ca. 1911. The Kobayashi family
ran a small inn in Lower Pā'ia. Nobuichi started one of the first auto repair businesses on Maui. After spending
time on O'ahu learning the automobile trade at Schuman Carriage, he returned to Maui and taught many others,
who later started their own repair businesses. Kobayashi's service station on Hāna Highway now houses
a windsurfing shop and other retail outlets. *Jim Fuller Collection*

13 **N. Kobayashi Auto Supply**
In his later years, "Kobe" Kobayashi presided over a service station filled with tools and car parts, wearing worn greasy coveralls and sharing sodas and stories with his customers. In the 1960s and '70s, his collection of parts and his knowledge of automobile repair helped many young people and newcomers keep their cars roadworthy.
Jim Fuller Collection

16 **Paia Clothes Cleaners**

One of the last of the old-time Pāʻia businesses, Paia Clothes Cleaners was founded in the 1920s by the Anzai family. It was passed down within the family, managed by twin brothers Gunji and Kunio Abe from 1968 to 1988. Today it is owned and operated by Gunji's daughter, Pauline, and her husband, Cliff Green. The laundry's original owners pose here ca. 1927. *Alexander & Baldwin Sugar Museum*

17 **Ikeda Store**
The Ikeda family made a success of their business by hard work and advertising. While his wife sewed and watched the store, Satoki Ikeda peddled clothes in the plantation camps. He posted English- and Japanese-language ads in community bathhouses and lured customers by nailing clothes up in his windows. Eventually, the Pā'ia store grew into a full-service clothing factory and expanded to the towns of Wailuku and Lahaina. The Pā'ia building, shown here in 1959, now houses a restaurant and various small businesses. *Wayne Tanaka Collection*

"A daring, broad daylight holdup..."

The Honolulu Star-Bulletin *called it "Hawaii's first bank robbery."* *This is how* The Maui News *described the Feb. 3, 1934, event:*

Less than five hours after $976.41 had been stolen from the Paia branch of Bank of Hawaii in a daring, broad daylight holdup, two Lahaina boys, George Wong, 18, and David Wong, 21, no kin, were in police custody and Monday were charged by Sheriff Clem C. Crowell with robbery, and most of the loot has been recovered.

All Maui was startled with the brazen effrontery of the boys, who drove up to the branch bank at 8:35 a.m. Saturday, waited until S.K. Yemoto and John D. Medeiros, tellers, were alone in the bank, and stalked in. While George Wong, who police believe is the instigator of the plot, held up the tellers with a .25 caliber automatic, David Wong allegedly scooped the money out of a drawer and off the top of the counter.

Getting into their car, which they had rented in Lahaina the day before, the boys removed the dark glasses they had been wearing, their ties and George wiped off the eyebrow pencil 'mustache' he had painted on his upper lip as a 'disguise.'

The boys drove up past the Paia hospital, then down the Hamakuapoko road to a point a few hundred yards from Maui high school where they changed clothes. David then turned the car around and drove up to Kula. George walked to a nearby Filipino camp and bummed a ride to Kahului.

David was driving past the Puunene hospital when he was arrested at 11:15 a.m. Saturday by detectives R. Quanson and John H. Waiwaiole.

David was taken to the Wailuku police headquarters where he was subjected to a stiff grilling by Sheriff Crowell. At 1 p.m., detectives R.A. Newton and Quanson arrested George walking the streets of Kahului.

Brought to the Wailuku police station, both boys confessed and had told police the complete story by 2 p.m. Saturday. Of the money, $934 was recovered, then turned over to Joaquin Garcia, assistant vice president of the Bank of Hawaii.

Beaming, Mr. Garcia said, "Thank you very much, sheriff. This is the best piece of work the Maui police have ever done."

The youthful Lahaina bandits were sentenced to 20 years in prison.
—The Maui News, Feb. 10, 1934

18 **Bank of Hawaii**

Organized in 1913 as First National Bank of Paia, this bank branch was the first on Maui to boast a concrete building on its own land. In 1917 this bank merged with those in Wailuku and Lahaina as Bank of Maui, Ltd. In 1930 Bank of Maui merged with the Bank of Hawaii. A few years later, it was the site of Maui's first bank robbery. Bank of Hawaii now is located in a new building farther down Baldwin Avenue, while this original structure is privately owned.

Bank of Hawaii

PAIA DEPOT

19 Paia Railroad Depot

Rail provided transportation for Maui's people and crops for many years. Kahului Railroad Co. laid tracks to Pā'ia in 1905, establishing the depot shown here ca. 1910. This railroad system, the oldest in Hawai'i, began with the first recorded Maui locomotive run in July 1879. After a series of owners, two railroads merged in 1899 into one, Kahului Railroad, under the control of Hawaiian Commercial & Sugar Co. KRR grew to encompass some 50 miles of track, several terminals and more than 250 cars. *Maui Historical Society*

19 **Paia Bus Depot**

By the time this photo was taken in the late 1930s, Kahului Railroad had introduced a bus line that replaced rail as transportation for the people of Central and East Maui. The railroad itself closed in 1966, following several years of unprofitable operations. Since then the depot building has housed several businesses, including a factory that made flowers and foliage into gold-plated jewelry and, after that, a windsurfing board manufacturer. *Ruth Mukai Collection*

19 **Railroad Family**

Soichi Okazaki was stationmaster of the Pā'ia depot when Kahului Railroad shifted from trains to buses for passenger transportation. He is shown here with his daughter Ruth ca. 1937. The Okazaki family lived in a large house behind the station. Ruth Mukai remembers riding the train to Ha'ikū just for fun. Other adults recall *kolohe* (mischievous) antics: kids smeared rails with guavas or grease to slow the trains and make it easier to hitch rides.

Ruth Mukai Collection

20 **Paia Mill**

Paia Mill was first established in 1880 to replace the original Paliuli mill, where sugar pioneers Henry Baldwin and Samuel Alexander ground raw cane in the early days of their first plantation. This new Maui Agricultural Co. Pāʻia factory, erected in 1906, replaced the old Hāmākuapoko plant built in 1879 for predecessor plantations in a complicated web of companies that eventually evolved into Hawaiian Commercial & Sugar Co. The Pāʻia mill still stands, though it stopped grinding cane in September 2000. *Maui Historical Society*

21 **Maui Agricultural Co.**
MACo. was formed in 1903 through the consolidation of Haiku Sugar Co., Paia Plantation and several other related companies. This building, which is now headquarters of East Maui Irrigation Co., was originally the main office for Paia Plantation and MACo. It was built in 1911, replacing an earlier headquarters that burned down. Alexander & Baldwin, Inc. heir Harry Baldwin worked out of an office here during the years he headed MACo.
Maui Historical Society

22 **First Hawaiian Bank**
Tall trees grew to shade the Maui Agricultural Co. building, and an extension was added to house a new bank.
Wailuku-based Baldwin Bank opened a Pā'ia branch in 1925 for the convenience of its Upcountry customers. In 1933
Baldwin Bank became Bishop First National Bank, then First Hawaiian Bank in 1969. Shown here in the early '70s,
the branch closed after plantation workers began moving to new population centers, and the building extension now
houses the Paia Farm division of Hawaiian Commercial & Sugar Co.. *Jim Fuller Collection*

23 Paia Store

Paia Store opened in 1896 to serve Paia Plantation workers and their families. Like other Pā'ia retailers, this main plantation-operated outlet did much of its business by sending peddlers to the camps and returning to deliver orders the next day. Plantation workers often charged their purchases, using a worker ID tag called a "bango" to obtain credit until payday. The original Paia Store burned down in 1910, along with the first Maui Agricultural Co. office, and this one was built to replace it. *Maui Historical Society*

34   Paia Store

One of the island's largest retailers, Paia Store also operated six branches in outlying camps for the convenience of plantation camp residents. The main store was organized by departments—men's furnishings, dry goods, Japanese foods and other goods. Bookkeeper Tom Dye and assistant manager Andrew Moodie pose here in 1941. The establishment closed in 1961, along with the other Hawaiian Commercial & Sugar Co. plantation stores. Today concrete steps across from Paia Mill still mark the old store's location. *Mary Moodie Collection/ Maui Historical Society*

24 Paia Hongwanji Mission

Founded in 1907, the Paia Hongwanji Mission built this temple in Nashiwa Camp ten years later. In pre-World War II days, Pā'ia's camps were said to have the largest number of Japanese plantation workers in Hawai'i. The mission provided religious and social activities and ran a Japanese Language School, which at one time boasted more than 1,000 students. As Pā'ia's population dwindled, however, the congregation relocated to the town of Makawao. Today, the Makawao Hongwanji is best known for its bazaar, held on the weekend of the town's annual Fourth of July rodeo.

Makawao Hongwanji Mission

25 **Holy Rosary Church**

Like several other Upcountry Catholic churches, Holy Rosary Church in Kū'au was built by Father James Beissel, who arrived on Maui in 1882. In 1926, this simple wood-frame church at the site of the Kū'au Catholic Cemetery was replaced by a more elaborate new concrete structure in Upper Pā'ia. Outside the church on Baldwin Avenue stands a statue honoring Father Damien De Veuster, who was beatified in 1995 in recognition of his work with leprosy patients at Kalaupapa on the island of Moloka'i.
Maui Historical Society

26 Paia School
Established in 1881 with William Cross Crook as its first teacher, Paia School was the first all-English-speaking school on Maui. It opened with an attendance of 20 pupils, mostly Hawaiian-speaking. To force his students to learn English, Crook decided not to learn Hawaiian himself. The 1909 building at far right burned in 1963, but the 1926 building at center still serves the Pā'ia area today. Ironically, it was at Paia School that Maui's first public school Hawaiian-immersion program began in 1988. *Alexander & Baldwin Sugar Museum*

27 **Paia Hospital**

Built in 1908 by Maui Agricultural Co., Paia Hospital was one of the largest, most up-to-date hospitals in the Territory of Hawai'i. It also introduced Maui's first ambulance in 1912. Paia Hospital was phased out in the late 1940s when a new HC&S hospital was built at Pu'unēnē in central Maui. In 1949 the old hospital reopened as the Maui Children's Home, which closed in 1965. Carpeted in sugar cane today, the hospital site is marked by a small monument on Baldwin Avenue below Makawao Union Church. *Alexander & Baldwin Sugar Museum*

28 Holomua Road

Cars line Holomua Road in this photo from the 1937 Maui High School annual. The school was located in Hāmākuapoko village, up Holomua Road from Ho'okipa Beach Park. "H'poko" was a busy place, with hundreds of residents, several churches, a store, a theater and a public school as well as Maui High School. Today, only the shell of Maui High School and a few adjacent buildings remain of this once-thriving village.

Maui High School Annual/ William Tavares Collection

CHAPTER TWO

Hāmākuapoko, Pa'uwela and Ha'ikū

29 **Maui High School**

Maui High opened at Hāmākuapoko in 1913 for 16 students and three teachers—a two-year high school that would serve Central and East Maui for 58 years. This ornate school building is shown in 1937, 16 years after it was erected. Many students rode the Kahului Railroad from as far away as Wailuku. Old Maui High was replaced in 1972 by a new school in Kahului. Some of the buildings in the old location continued in use, for projects such as the study of nitrogen fixation in agriculture.

Maui High School Annual / William Tavares Collection

29 May Fete at Maui High

Queen Sylvia Johnson presides over her court at the 1937 May Fete at the old Hāmākuapoko campus. Many of Maui's future leaders graduated from the school; one of them, Patsy Takemoto Mink, went on to a political career that took her to the U.S. House of Representatives. While the old school is now in ruins, it is still possible to drive down Holomua Road, turning off Baldwin Avenue just above the Paia Hospital monument and exiting on Hāna Highway near Hoʻokipa Beach Park. *Maui High School Annual / William Tavares Collection*

30 **Pauwela Store**

Three Pa'uwela stores served pineapple workers from Haiku Fruit & Packing Co.—which became Haiku Pineapple Co. in 1928—and Libby, McNeill & Libby. The store at this corner was built by a Chinese businessman named Yap ca. 1900. Later it was known as Akiona Store. From 1972 to 1975 electronics specialist Steve Rose and Pa'uwela resident John Manner Franco ran Keone and Steve's Reasonable Store at the site, with an inventory of basic food items and surplus electronics that brought neighborhood old-timers and newcomers together. *Hawai'i State Archives*

31 **Kuiaha Gulch**

A Kahului Railroad train crosses the trestle over Kuiaha Gulch in 1963, just three years before the railroad finally shut down operations. This trestle was part of a railway extension to the Pauwela Pineapple Cannery completed in 1925. Trains delivered fresh pineapple from land in Kahakuloa that the company acquired in 1922, and carried its canned products to Kahului Harbor. *David Cup Choy Collection*

32 Haserot Cannery

Shown here in 1964, the Haserot Cannery was launched in 1919 as the Pauwela Pineapple Co. It was the fourth cannery built on Maui; three of them including Haserot were located in the prime growing area around Haʻikū. In 1926, Libby, McNeill & Libby took over the company, and Henry Haserot bought out Libby's interest in 1963. Haserot shut down a decade later, however, driven out of business like other Hawaiʻi growers by foreign competition. The Pauwela Cannery building now houses various light industrial and retail businesses. *David Cup Choy Collection*

35 Haiku Fruit & Packing Co.
Hawai'i's pineapple industry began on Maui in 1890 at Ha'ikū, when D.D. Baldwin began experimenting with plantings. He shipped his first fresh pineapples to San Francisco in 1900, and the Haiku Fruit & Packing Co. was incorporated three years later. The cannery, shown here ca. 1920, was built in 1904. By the '20s it was the largest and most complete plant of its kind on Maui. A windstorm destroyed much of the building in the 1970s, and its foundation is now a parking lot for the Haiku Marketplace. *Maui Historical Society*

Life in the Country

Before World War II changed life in Hawai'i forever, the little village of Ha'ikū was the commercial center of a large agricultural area. Maui's first pineapple cannery, Haiku Fruit & Packing Co., had begun operations in 1903, and independent farmers for miles around brought their fruit there to be processed. Near the cannery at the corner of Ha'ikū and Kokomo Roads were the Haiku General Store, a bank and a doctor's office. The Watanabe General Store & Garage had a stage in its garage where, in the 1930s, there were *kabuki* shows, films, parties and political rallies.

Emily Baldwin Young grew up in the Haiku House, originally built for the manager of Haiku Sugar Co., and later the home of several generations of the Baldwin family. Two yardmen cared for the 23 acres of lawn and trees surrounding the house.

Just downhill, Haiku Farm was a going concern, and C.H. "Buster" Burnett ran his chicken farm in the area. A big mango orchard had been planted nearby by William Baldwin. "There was a little farm camp," Emily Young recalls, "and my playmates were all children from the camp. My father had a huge feedlot for his cattle. He'd bring them from Kaupo Ranch and fatten them in the pastures there. He was the first rancher on the island to use pine bran as a food supplement."

Emily sometimes played on a wooden horse her father had built for polo practice. Complete with a saddle, it was set into a court he'd designed so that balls he hit rolled back to be hit again.

But this peaceful rural life was about to change. The cannery closed in 1938 and when war came to the Pacific three years later, Maui became a training ground. Up the road, Marines camped in the pastures of Kokomo. One of the bachelor dormitories formerly used by cannery workers became an officers' club. Today, Ha'ikū's pastures are dotted with new houses, and the dorm building has become a school, Horizons Academy.

33 Haiku House
The little trees in the foreground of this photo have long since grown to be giants, part of a grove on Ha'ikū Road filled with varieties both common and rare. In the late 1800s the house was the home of the manager of Haiku Sugar Co., whose mill was just across the road. Henry P. and Emily Baldwin later lived there, then their son William, followed by William's son, Dwight H. Baldwin. After Dwight's death in the 1960s it was sold and dubbed "Baldwin Manor" by a subsequent owner, but the Baldwin family always called it "Haiku House." *Emily Young Collection*

34 **Bank of Hawaii**
The Ha'ikū branch of Bank of Hawaii was built next to the Haiku Store in 1931 and included space for a post office. Ha'ikū was then a busy little village serving the people of the agricultural district stretching from Huelo to Hāmākuapoko. Just across the way, Haiku Pineapple Co. canned fruit grown by independent farmers. Today, the intersection of Kokomo and Ha'ikū Roads is still the commercial center for this rural area. The old bank building was restored in 1998 and now houses a delicatessen. *Alice Texeira Collection / Courtesy Lafayette Young*

36 Camp Maui
The men of the
4th Marine Division
are perhaps the
best remembered
of the thousands
of military people
who served on
Maui during World
War II. They were
stationed at Camp
Maui in Kokomo,
in pastureland
where they rested
between brutal
battles in the
Pacific. They were
entertained in
private homes and
at USO dances,
and they practiced
their battle skills in
East Maui's bamboo
forests and their
amphibious landings
on the beaches of
Kīhei. Camp Maui
is now the site of
a park honoring
"Maui's Marines."
Maui Historical Society

48 **Polo in Makawao**
With a string of his beloved polo ponies, rancher Oskie Rice stands in a pasture above Makawao, below the rodeo arena that now bears his name. With him are cowboy Ben Kekiwi, at right, and Kenji Ikeda, described by Oskie's son Henry as "the best jockey Maui ever saw." The pasture, across from Poʻokela Church, still looks much as it did when this photo was taken ca. 1935. *Kaonoulu Ranch*

CHAPTER THREE
Makawao

54

37 **Makawao Union Church**

Maunaolu Female Seminary students pose with congregation members at Makawao Union Church. The church, chartered in 1861, was first headquartered in a building at what is now the site of the Makawao Cemetery. The frame structure shown here was built in 1889 closer to Pāʻia, on the spot where an early Alexander & Baldwin sugar mill had stood. It, in turn, was replaced in 1917, when the Baldwin family erected the existing stone building in honor of Henry Perrine Baldwin, one of A&B's founders and a longtime church organist.

Makawao Union Church

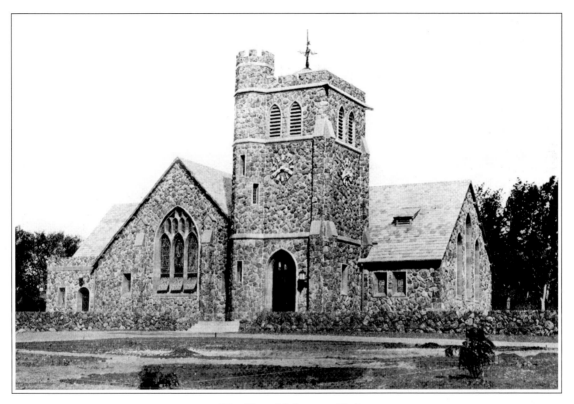

37 **New Makawao Union**

An Upcountry landmark, today's Makawao Union was built near the boundaries of Upper Pāʻia in 1917. It was designed by the celebrated Hawaiʻi architect C.W. Dickey, in basically Gothic style in the manner of an English village church. Its interior of American white oak is illuminated by stained glass windows transferred from the old church. Makawao Union Church is on both the Hawaiʻi and National Registers of Historic Places. *Makawao Union Church*

38 Paia Community House

In 1911 the congregation of Makawao Union Church built a community hall which has been in continuous use ever since. Known as the Paia Community House, it has provided space for bazaars, dances, wedding receptions and plays. For the annual bazaars, plantation carpenters built separate booths where the ladies sold handcrafts and baked goods; one year, two pretty teachers ran a kissing booth, charging a dollar a kiss. In this photo taken on March 16, 1918, the cast of *Chimes of Normandy* poses on the stage that still exists today. *Makawao Union Church*

39 **Fred Baldwin Memorial Home**
After their young son, Frederick Chambers Baldwin, died in 1905, H.P. and Emily Baldwin founded the Fred Baldwin Memorial Home to house indigent and infirm old men. The building became a hospital during World War II, reopened for its elderly residents afterwards and was closed in 1958. Its charitable work was shifted to the Fred Baldwin Memorial Foundation. Maui Land & Pineapple Co. now houses seasonal workers in the building, located on Baldwin Avenue between Mauna'olu and the Makawao Union Church. *Maui Land & Pineapple Co.*

40 Maunaolu Seminary
Founded in 1861 as a girls' school, the East Maui Female Seminary became known as Maunaolu Seminary (*mauna'olu*—"pleasant mountain"). The original building in Makawao was destroyed by fire in 1869, and a new one that replaced it also burned in 1898. Today's building, shown here, was completed in 1900, a gift from Henry P. Baldwin. In 1942 the school became a military hospital and headquarters, and in 1950 it became Maunaolu Community College, Maui's first institution of higher learning. *Maui Historical Society*

40 **Maunaolu Community College**
The student body was coed by the time the old Maunaolu Seminary became Maunaolu Community College. Students are shown here in 1954 at the turnoff to the school, which offered the last two years of high school and the first two years of college. By 1964 it was a fully accredited, coeducational two-year college with more than 200 students, but it soon had a formidable rival in Maui Community College. It closed in 1964, having graduated only one four-year class, nicknamed the "Edsel Class." The campus is now a Hawaii Job Corps location. *Wayne Tanaka Collection*

4I **Kaluanui**

Kaluanui, once the graceful estate of Harry and Ethel Baldwin, was built near the remains of one of Maui's earliest sugar mills. Run by mule power, this mill had been the first in Hawai'i to use centrifugal force for separating sugar crystals. Two of Maui's largest hybrid Cook and Norfolk Island pine trees can still be found near the house. Today, the ten-acre estate, pictured here in the 1920s, is home to the Hui No'eau Visual Arts Center, which offers art exhibits and classes in an array of disciplines. *Hui No'eau Visual Arts Center*

41 **Kaluanui**

The spacious Mediterranean-style home was designed for the Baldwins in 1917 by the noted Hawai'i architect C.W. Dickey. In 1976, the late Colin Cameron—the Baldwins' grandson—granted usage of Kaluanui to the visual arts center. In addition to the stucco house at the end of a tree-lined driveway off Baldwin Avenue, the property today encompasses original outbuildings now used for ceramics, printmaking, papermaking and woodworking.

Hui No'eau Visual Arts Center

41 | Harry A. Baldwin

H.A. Baldwin, son of Alexander & Baldwin founder Henry P. Baldwin, sits astride one of his beloved horses outside the stables at his home, Kaluanui, in the 1940s. An animal lover, Baldwin was especially fond of horses and rode frequently. Harry Baldwin, who succeeded his father as one of the most powerful men on Maui, was head of several family businesses and also served in the Territorial Senate and as Hawai'i's delegate to the U.S. Congress.

Haleakala Ranch

41 **Ethel Baldwin**

Ethel Smith Baldwin, born in Honolulu in 1879, showed a love of the arts from early childhood. In 1934 Ethel, her daughter Frances and a small group of friends founded Hui Noʻeau "to stimulate an appreciation for the arts in Maui County." Ethel painted in a bright upstairs room, used a small cottage behind the main house as a jewelry studio and often invited friends to work with her. Artistic talent still runs in the family: Ethel's great-granddaughter Claire Sanford won the Best in Show award at a Hui Noʻeau juried exhibit in 2001.

Mary Cameron Sanford

42 **Kitada Kau Kau Korner**
Takeshi and Suteko Kitada stand with their children—from left, Nobuko, Etsuko and Tsuyoshi—outside their store and restaurant in 1952. The Kitadas opened the restaurant in 1947 and later offered merchandise as a retail store. Today, Kitada's is a restaurant where folks still stop in for an old-fashioned local-style breakfast or lunch. Kitada's hasn't changed much over the years, except that Takeshi and Suteko have passed on, leaving daughter Nobu in charge.

Nobuko Kitada Collection

Komoda Store
Takezo Komoda
started his store and
bakery about 1916,
on the site now
occupied by Polli's
Mexican Restaurant.
In the 1940s he
relocated across
the intersection
of Baldwin and
Makawao Roads to
the current Komoda
Store and Bakery
location, shown
here in the early
'50s. From Makawao
landowner Rose
Crook, Komoda
purchased first the
lot and later the
parcel next door
for a parking lot.
Betty Komoda
Shibuya, who
manages the store
today, is the child
at left in this
photograph.
Komoda Family Collection

"Molina asked what the horse wanted to drink..."

The history of the building that today houses Casanova Italian Restaurant and Deli exemplifies the transformation of Makawao in the 20th Century. In its early days, this was the Tam Chow Store, owned by one of the Chinese immigrants who set up shop in the small Upcountry town in the 1920s and '30s. When World War II began, the building was converted to a USO facility, done up in ranch style appropriate to the surrounding area.

After the war, Makawao followed the rest of the island into economic doldrums. In 1951 Helen Tam, owner of the Tam Chow Store, sold the building to Salvador "Sub" Molina, who with his wife, Mary, ran a small liquor store on Baldwin Avenue. It reopened in 1952 as Club Rodeo, a liquor store, bar and nightclub. Its new owner and his family worked hard to make a go of it. They opened a chicken farm on the premises, and the Molina kids cleaned eggs every morning before they set off for school. Sub Molina not only ran the business, from bartending to floor mopping, but played saxophone with his brothers in the popular Molina Brothers Orchestra.

Eventually Club Rodeo became an Upcountry institution. Local cowboys used the place to organize the Maui Roping Club, sponsor of the annual Fourth of July Makawao Rodeo. After a grand opening in 1963, the bar became a restaurant, and families came to enjoy prime rib and Portuguese bean soup. Molina sold the chickens. One memorable day, an out-of-town cowboy rode his horse through town looking for the annual rodeo, spotted the Club Rodeo sign and rode right up the steps into the restaurant. Molina simply asked him what the horse wanted to drink.

The Molinas sold Club Rodeo in 1976, and the building went through a succession of incarnations. In 1978, the owner of Longhi's restaurant in Lahaina bought it, bringing gourmet food and rock concerts. Later it became a Mexican restaurant, then the Italian Piero's, and then Casanova. Though the crowd had become more yuppie than cowboy, and the food now had a European flavor, the old building at Makawao's main crossroads was still a social center, and one could still see the local Portuguese cowboys in their jeans and boots, gathered at the bar.

44 **Club Rodeo**
It was a big day when Club Rodeo opened anew as a restaurant in 1963. The grand opening included a parade through Makawao and guests of honor such as U.S. Senator Daniel Inouye and Maui County Chairman Eddie Tam. The restaurant would become so popular that, on one busy Fourth of July weekend, owner Sub Molina had to drive around town begging to borrow chairs so he could seat all of his customers. *Molina Family Collection*

45 **Crossroads USO**

During the war, servicemen flocked to the Crossroads USO, where they found books, a pool table and ping pong room, desks and card tables, a piano and that indispensable ingredient wherever young men gather: young women. After the war, the Molina family turned the building into Club Rodeo, famous for its Portuguese bean soup and prime rib. It has housed several restaurants since Club Rodeo closed, including the current Casanova Italian Restaurant.

Mary Cameron Sanford

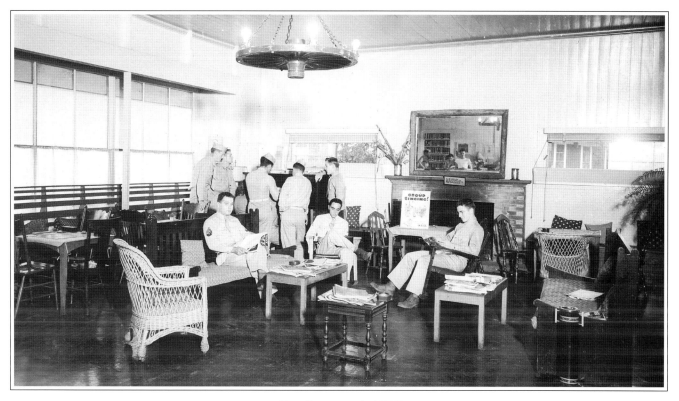

45 **Crossroads USO**

In 1943 Ethel Baldwin started the Crossroads USO in the former Tam Chow Store to provide a place of recreation for the thousands of service members who spent part of World War II on Maui. The historic building was decorated in ranch motif: Barrels were turned into desks and seats, tin cans with horseshoes attached became ashtrays, old wagon wheels became chandeliers. The color scheme was dominated by Ethel Baldwin's trademark "practical brown."

Mary Cameron Sanford

45 Crossroads Service

A Makawao landmark for many years, this service station belonged to Hajime Karakawa for at least 30 years before he sold it to Joseph Tam Sing in 1962. The station, like many Makawao businesses, was on land previously owned by the Crook family, for whom Joseph Tam Sing worked as a bookkeeper. Tam Sing turned it over to his sons, Dickie and Jimmy. The station closed in 1983 and is now the site of several retail shops. *Jimmy Tam Sing Collection*

46, 50 **Makawao Post Office**
Postmaster Emil "Bill" Balthazar answers the phone at the post office in 1962. He was one of Upcountry's best-known residents during his four decades as postmaster, from 1949 until his death in 1988. In 1950 Balthazar opened a new post office in a wooden building at the rear of the parking lot that now serves Casanova Restaurant. Today, that old post office is the home of Mauka Physical Therapy, while Makawao's post office is run by Balthazar's daughter, Celine, in a new facility built in 1980. A bridge on Makawao Avenue near Brewer Road is named for Emil Balthazar.
Wayne Tanaka Collection

The Crook Family of Makawao

The Crook family left a legacy to the town of Makawao and in the minds of Maui's children.

William Cross Crook, born in England in 1828, arrived in Hawai'i in 1880, when the islands were under the reign of King Kalākaua. He was assigned to teach at Pā'ia, where Henry P. Baldwin was then the school agent.

"Mr. Baldwin told me my schoolhouse was not yet finished and sent me to his residence at Sunnyside with a note to Mrs. Baldwin to give me a room. That evening he told me the building would not be ready for a month so the following day I returned to Wailuku to await its completion," Crook recalled in 1922.

While he waited, Crook had visited other schools where both Hawaiian and English languages were taught. Crook's school was to be an English-only institution, the first on Maui. In January 1881 the schoolhouse opened with three rooms and seats for 60 students.

While most of his students could read and write Hawaiian, they knew no English, which was a problem when Baldwin informed Crook that the children must be ready to give an "exhibition" by the beginning of summer vacation. Crook solved the problem by having them memorize speaking pieces and songs, even though they did not understand the words.

Crook talked Baldwin into building a teacher's cottage, the first on Maui. He later acquired land and a house in Makawao. His wife, Mary, and at least one child, Rose "Nellie," also worked in the schools. William Crook lived to be 96 and was still spry and teaching well into his 80s.

His daughter Rose was a well-known Makawao resident in the early 20th Century. The family at one time owned a large portion of Makawao town and over the years parceled it out to new owners. Miss Crook, as she was commonly called, sold one lot to Takezo Komoda for $10 in 1945. Komoda then moved from his original location across the street to this current site of the celebrated T. Komoda Store and Bakery.

Miss Crook died in 1962, remembered fondly for her generosity and her wonderful garden of roses, grapes and rare passion fruit. A remnant of the Crook estate remains, a private green oasis of towering trees awaiting a use worthy of its history.

47 Crook Camp

William C. Crook, at right, is shown with his daughter, Rose, and an unidentified man outside their Makawao home. The pine tree in the background is believed to be the one that still towers above the town, just behind Komoda Store. Crook, a pioneering educator who for years was principal of Paia School, owned a large part of Makawao town, and the private estate surrounding his former home is still called Crook Camp by many old-timers.

Jimmy Tam Sing Collection

51 **Hardy House**

Makawao School principal Frederick Hardy stands with his son, Hollis, in front of the house he and his wife, Lillian, built when they married in 1897. When Hardy died in 1920, Lillian sold the house and its 20 acres. Subsequent owners added on to the building and sold all but half an acre of the land. Ernest and Alene Rezents bought the house at the corner of Makawao and Kealaloa Avenues in 1961. They have since continued to work on its restoration, and in 1984 this private residence was listed on both the State and National Registers of Historic Places. *Rezents Family Collection*

49 **Saint Joseph Church**
Priests stand outside St. Joseph Church in Makawao, built in 1911. A bell tower was added in 1927. The original St. Joseph Church was housed in a small frame structure on the site above the cemetery, next to the present building. It was built by Father James Beissel, a German priest who arrived in Makawao in 1882 and built at least a half-dozen churches Upcountry, including Holy Ghost in Kula. Saint Joseph's traditional annual carnival has always included a feature appropriate to ranch country: a livestock auction.
Marciel Family Collection

A Ranch in the House of the Sun

Attaining Paradise in the hereafter does not concern me greatly. I was born in Paradise...

...The ranch where we lived bore the proud name of the great volcano on which it sprawled—Haleakala, The House of the Sun. Impressively simple in outline, like all Hawaiian volcanoes, wrapped in loneliness and mystery, the quiescent giant brooded like an aloof god guarding our world. The sixty thousand acres of throbbing soil, forming the ranch, sat like a mammoth saddle on the back of the ten-thousand-foot mountain. In places the land was robed with rich jungles, elsewhere it was scarred by black lava which had once streamed in molten scarlet to the sea. From the shimmering grasslands and eucalyptus groves at Makawao, at the two-thousand-foot level, rolling hills and cattle-dotted pastures went up to the summit of Haleakala. Down through the livid scar of the crater, up the battlements of the far rim, then down the far slope of the mountain, the wide acres poured like a green torrent to the sea....

...Like most Island-born children I always woke early, sensing a vague, pleasurable stir in the atmosphere long before light welled into the sky. I knew as I lay in bed listening to wind prowling down from Haleakala that the stars outside the open windows were subtly changing. I knew grazing stock were raising their heads for an instant in their salute to the unending wonder of light being born out of darkness. Ah Sin was stealing into the kitchen, the lantern he carried making great shadows, like opening and shutting scissors, as his legs moved. Presently the smell of kerosene being poured on a wood fire and lighted drifted through the house, followed by the sound of coffee being ground and the swift rush of water in Dad's shower.

Then, mysteriously, from being just a small girl, I was transformed into an atom of the wide splendid life about me. Shivers of pleasure, mingled with anticipation for the royal new day being born, chased over me as I listened to whips cracking, the rush of horses' hoofs in the pastures and snatches of hulas being sung as men went about the great business of a sixty-thousand-acre ranch.

— *from* Born In Paradise *by Armine von Tempski*

52 Haleakala Ranch

Horse trainer and jockey Benny Rollins came to Hawai'i from Ireland and spent many years caring for racehorses and ranch stallions at Haleakala Ranch. He is shown here mounted in the late 1930s, accompanied by ranch workers Apela De Rego and Tommy Yusaka, Sr. The ranch purchased horses from Parker Ranch on the Big Island of Hawai'i and raced them at the track at Kahului, Maui. Ranch Manager Richard "Manduke" Baldwin's wife, Haku, directed training during the 1940s.

Haleakala Ranch

54 **Haleakala Polo Field**

Introduced to Maui by Haleakala Ranch Manager Louis von Tempsky around 1900, polo flourished in Upcountry fields until World War II. After the war, Haku Baldwin began training youngsters from the ranch, re-establishing Maui's riders as dominant polo players in Hawai'i. Here at the Haleakala Polo Field ca. 1950 are, left to right, Stanley Woolaway, Samuel Lyons, Peter Baldwin, Bennet Baldwin, referee Arthur Perkins, Henry Rice, Bill Baldwin, Mike Lyons and Allen Sakamoto. Polo is still played at this field. *Haleakala Ranch*

53 Haleakala Herefords

The first Herefords imported to Haleakala Ranch were lined up for a photo soon after their arrival in the 1920s. The ranch was founded in 1888 by a partnership that included Lorrin A. Thurston and H.P. Baldwin. In 1896, Haleakala Ranch added a dairy, placing its milking barn at the site of the pen shown here. More than 30,000 acres in ranch lands included, at one time, Haleakalā Crater. Ranch headquarters is still located across from the site of this pen above Makawao, beneath towering eucalyptus trees planted a century ago by Louis von Tempsky.

Haleakala Ranch

53 Haleakala Roundup

Cowboys round up Haleakala Ranch calves for branding, as the animals' mothers bawl on the other side of the fence. In the 1940s these cowboys still used the traditional braided leather ropes called *kaula 'ili*. The fencing in the background is made of narrow-gauge rail. Today, Haleakala Ranch includes 32,000 acres, and its cowboys still manage herds on horseback.

Milton Holst / Haleakala Ranch

53 **Branding at Haleakala Ranch**
In the 1940s a cowboy holding a de-horning tool stands over a calf whose hide still smokes from branding. At left, a horseman carefully keeps the rope taut, immobilizing the calf. Horns were pulled to protect other cattle, as well as the cowboys and their horses. Tar was smeared on the wound after the horn was removed. Today, cattle on Maui's ranches are bred to be hornless.
Milton Holst / Haleakala Ranch

55 Keāhua Bon Dance

Some of Maui's first Japanese *bon* dances took place at Keāhua Camp, now replaced by cane fields below the town of Pukalani. Here in 1924 members of the Keāhua Fukushima Ondo group are seated by the village *yagura*, or musicians' tower. On the tower, second from left, is Tomio Watanabe, whose family has played *taiko* drums at Maui *bon* dances since the turn of the century. Tomio was a second-generation Mauian; today three members of the family's fifth Maui generation still perform at these traditional memorial services for the dead. *Watanabe Family Collection*

Chapter Four
Hāliʻimaile and Keāhua

55 Keahua Japanese School

Youngsters in Keāhua Camp attended Japanese language classes after their English school ended each day, at the combination school and recreation center shown in this early-20th-Century photo. Until the teacher rang the bell for Japanese school to start, they would play games outside, using such makeshift equipment as a volleyball fashioned from crumpled newspaper and wrapped with string. *Watanabe Family Collection*

55 Keahua School Graduation

This 1940 graduating class of Keahua Japanese School was one of the last to study the Japanese language in the old school. After the war in the Pacific began the following year, Japanese language schools were closed for the duration. Within a few years of the war's end in 1945, Keāhua and other plantation camps began to shut down as Alexander & Baldwin offered homes in its new "Dream City" at Kahului. Then a little town of several hundred, with a church, public school and store, Keāhua is no more. *Watanabe Family Collection*

55 **Waiakoa Nursery School**

The signs identify this as Waiakoa Nursery on Paia Plantation. There was a Waiakoa Camp when this picture was taken in 1913, and it is possible the camp operated a nursery for mothers who spent their days in the fields. Waiakoa, however, was officially part of the Makawao Plantation, which like Paia Plantation was owned by Maui Agricultural Co. The family who owns this photo lived in Keāhua, so perhaps the nursery was actually in Keāhua and the "Waiakoa" in the name had nothing to do with the location. *Watanabe Family Collection*

55   **Molina Brothers Orchestra**
The music of the young Molina Brothers Orchestra was a familiar sound in the village of Keāhua, where they practiced
in the family home. For more than two decades, beginning in the mid-'30s, the orchestra was Maui's top dance band.
Shown here are John on drums; Joseph on banjo; Rafael, Domingo, Henry and Salvador on sax; Antonio on piano;
Frank on bass; and Manuel (standing, with no instrument). *Domingo Molina Collection*

56 Haliimaile Store

The old plantation store that served Maui Land & Pineapple's Haliimaile Plantation became the Haliimaile Super Market, and included a post office at left front, here in the early '60s. The cinder blocks used to build the post office extension were made by the pineapple company. The post office has since been demolished, and in 1992 the building became the popular Hali'imaile General Store restaurant. *Maui Land & Pineapple Co.*

57 **Haliimaile Plantation Office**

This office at Hāli'imaile was built in 1932 and expanded in 1955. The original corporate headquarters for Maui Land & Pineapple Co., it also included the office of company president J. Walter Cameron. The building is still in use, still much as it was in Cameron's day. Its two Italian cypress trees *(left)*—removed due to disease—were an area landmark in their day. *Maui Land & Pineapple Co.*

62 **Kula Botanical Garden**

Warren McCord plants Monterey pines, the first of the Christmas tree farm at Kula Botanical Garden, as daughter Carolyn looks on. A tourist attraction and a favorite stop for Mauians at Christmas, this six-acre public garden features proteas, orchids, bromeliads and native plants along landscaped paths. The McCord family started the garden in 1968, carving out paths, waterfalls and ponds; building bridges and rest areas; and collecting plant specimens from around the world. *Kula Botanical Garden*

CHAPTER FIVE
Kula

63, 64 Waiohuli Pen

John S. Walker *(top left)* signs over Kaonoulu Ranch to Harold W. Rice, during a celebratory gathering at the ranch's Waiohuli Pen in August 1916. The man at center is notary Edgar Morton, and the car is a Cadillac. The ranch stretched in the manner of a traditional Hawaiian *ahupua'a* (land division) down the mountain to the shoreline at Kīhei. It was part of extensive land-holdings belonging to Rice, a progressive cattle and horse breeder who was elected a Territorial senator in 1918. The Rice family still rides the range on the slopes of Haleakalā today.

Kaonoulu Ranch

63 **Upcountry**
Paniolo
Grubby and grinning, five *paniolo* (Hawaiian cowboys) pause after a day of branding at Kaonoulu Ranch. The five are, left to right, Oskie Rice, Johnny Walker, Robert "Red" Chapman, Freddie Rice and young Henry Rice. Henry, the son of Oskie and grandson of Harold W. Rice, still runs Kaonoulu as a working cattle ranch.
Kaonoulu Ranch

58 **Pulehu Chapel**

In 1851 the first Hawaii mission of the Church of Jesus Christ of Latter-day Saints was established at Pūlehu by George Q. Cannon, who performed Maui's first Mormon baptism there. Cannon also translated the Book of Mormon into Hawaiian after his arrival on Maui in 1850. Shown here in the 1880s, Pulehu Chapel is still open to visitors.
Boyd Mossman Collection

59 **Old Morihara Store**
The Morihara family began their store in the 1930s when they lived in Camp One in Spreckelsville.
They later moved their operation to Waiakoa, Kula, where they lived over the store in the building shown here.
The store was moved once again to the former Tavares Meat and Grocery, and in 1981 the Moriharas bought
that building from the Tavares family. Morihara Store is still in business there. The original Kula store seen
here is now a private residence across from the Kula Community Center. *David Morihara Collection*

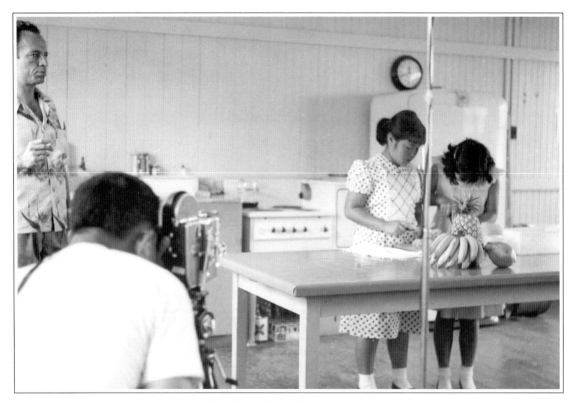

60 Kula Extension Service

Two young 4-H members demonstrate a recipe for the cameras of the KMVI-TV show, "Maui Story," a feature of the local television station launched by Maui Publishing Co. in 1955. KMVI announcer Robert Frost is seen at left. The University Extension Service building still stands behind the Kula Community Center in Waiakoa, where it is used by the Maui County Farm Bureau.

Dan Shigeta/University Extension Service Collection

60 Kula Farmers

Kula is famous for flower growing. Here in the 1960s Kula farmers show off chrysanthemum plants at the Sakuma farm in Upper Kula: *(left to right)* Kazu Suehisa, Tokio Watanabe, Azushi Sakuma and Yukio Matsui. For many years Kula was filled with colorful fields of carnations, often used to make fat carnation leis. More recently, as carnations succumbed to imported pests and diseases, the area has become notable for its exotic protea blooms.

Dan Shigeta/University Extension Service Collection

61 Holy Ghost Church

The people of Kula's Portuguese community pose during construction of booth framework for their annual Pentecost feast. The church, built in 1894 on land bought from Louis von Tempsky's Erehwon Ranch for just $24, has staged the feast each year since about 1885. Within the church are an altar and statues shipped from Austria in 1897, then hauled by oxcart from Kahului Harbor to Kula. The church and its priceless interior decorations were restored in 1994.

Kula Roman Catholic Community

65 St. John's Episcopal Church Nearly a century after it was built by Chinese immigrants, St. John's continues to serve its community today. This 1967 photo captures the beauty of the Kēōkea area where the church and the rectory (built in 1960) perch on the side of Haleakalā. St. John's has twice been led by women: by Father Shim Yin Chin's widow, Kui Kyau Shim, from 1923 to 1944, and, since 1981, by the Rev. Heather Mueller-Fitch (one of the first women ordained as a priest in the Episcopal Church). *St. John's Episcopal Church*

CHAPTER SIX
Kēōkea and 'Ulupalakua

65 St. John's Episcopal Church

St. John's Church is shown in 1910, with the original rectory at right. Parts of the wood-frame building were floated off a boat that arrived down the mountain at Mākena Landing and transported by horse-drawn carts to Kēōkea. The church was built in 1906 under the leadership of Father Shim Yin Chin, who raised $2,000 on Maui and Oʻahu to finance construction. It originally served as both a church and a Chinese language school. The rectory was moved down the road in 1960 and is now a private residence. *St. John's Episcopal Church*

67 Haleakala Hawaiian Church

Built in 1853, the church is shown here in 1949 from the vantage point of the St. John's Episcopal Church rectory. The house between the two churches is the Wong family's. The congregation of Haleakala Hawaiian allowed fledgling St. John's Church to use the building for special events—such as the visit of a bishop—before St. John's was completed in 1906. High winds destroyed the Haleakala Hawaiian Church roof in 1982. Today, a reactivated congregation is meeting in the church's shell and making plans to restore it. *St. John's Episcopal Church*

The Chinese in Kula

It was in the early years of this decade, 1910–1920, while we were still on the old farm, when news arrived that Dr. Sun Yat-Sen had dethroned the Manchu Dynasty on Oct. 10, 1911, and founded the Chinese Republic of China. Every Chinese in Kula, especially the Hakkas, were overjoyed, and to commemorate the occasion, a parade was held starting from Keokea to Kamaole, passing every farmer's house and down to Hop Wo Store, then back to Keokea again. There were people on horseback carrying Dr. Sun Yat-Sen's banner and the flags of China, and there were some on foot carrying musical instruments. Everywhere the parade went they were greeted with cheers and firecrackers. We kids were so excited, and we would join in the parade too. We had not seen or knew what a parade was until now. Upon reaching back to Keokea there were entertainment, feasting, drinking, and everybody was having a wonderful time. By now I was in my 11th year and I can say it was one of my fondest memories during this decade....

My closest neighbors were the Thompsons, the Mortons, the Santos and the Malias. Every time we wanted to have some fun and do some hell raising, we would saddle up and head for the mountains, rope a few bull calves, castrate them and turn them loose again and then pick up a couple more that is nice and fat and bring them home to slaughter. We would have fresh beef, salt beef and jerk beef for the house all year-round. There was any amount of wild cattle up in this mountain, and nobody owns them. If we are looking for fresh pork, mutton or for our Thanksgiving or Christmas dinners, we would shoot them with shotguns; however if we wanted them alive we would snare them by the dozens. When pheasant season came around we would use hunting dogs to hunt for them with a shotgun. If you crave for fresh fish, just saddle up, take your throw net and a few lines, then head for the beach. Before the night is over, you would get a couple of uluas on your line and by morning take a few throws with your net and you will have a bag of fish.

— *Willie Fong, 1978 oral history*

68 **Kwock Hing Society**

Members of the Kula Chinese community gather on the steps of the Kwock Hing Society, also known as the Ket Hing Society, for the 1931 visit of China's Consul General, King-Chau Mui. The first two-story structure in Kula, the society building was erected in 1907. It was a favorite gathering place for Chinese to eat, drink, gamble and share news of current events back in the old country. The original structure no longer exists, but its replacement stands on this same site on Cross Road.
St. John's Episcopal Church

Chinese Families

The son of Chinese immigrants, Willie Fong—shown here with son Harry in 1917—led an adventuresome life in the pioneer farming and ranching area of Kēōkea. The Fong family lived in the thriving Chinese community between ʻUlupalakua and Kēōkea and survived later economic downturns and social changes to remain in Kula. Other Chinese families still living in the area include the Hews, Shims, Chings, Wongs and Chungs.

St. John's Episcopal Church

66 **Keokea School**

Francis S.C. Fong stands outside Keokea School in 1937, when its student body numbered about 150. Keokea began as a one-room school in 1890. Most of its students were Chinese, who often attended Chinese school before and after their English lessons. Keokea closed in 1964, when it was consolidated with three other Kula schools to form Kula Elementary. An old teachers' cottage near St. John's Episcopal Church is all that remains of Keokea School.

St. John's Episcopal Church

69 Fong Store
Henry S. Fong Store & Service Station today looks much the same as it did here ca. 1940s. Fong also ran a theater next door, which opened in 1936 with a showing of *Petrified Forest*. Kahului Railroad Co. buses carried movie fans from other districts for the grand opening. The theater is no longer standing, but Fong Store and its neighbor, the K.S. Ching Store, founded in 1937, are still open for business. *Fong Family Collection*

69 **Fong Store**

Violet Hew Fong presides over a thriving grocery business in this 1942 photo. The store on Kula Highway opened in 1932, having moved down the hill from the original Fong Store started in 1908 and run by Harry Foon Seong Fong. Violet was married to Harry's brother, Henry, who took over the store when Harry died. When storekeeping grew unprofitable during the Great Depression, Henry began a contracting business that eventually became Fong Construction. *Fong Family Collection*

70 **Old Kula Sanitarium**

In the beginning, the Kula County Farm and Sanitarium, established in 1910 to care for victims of tuberculosis, housed its patients in tents. After a couple of storms, that flimsy setup was replaced by these wooden cottages. A Preventorium opened in 1926 to stop the spread of the disease among underweight children, who were brought to live in a "fresh air camp" on the sanitarium grounds and fed nourishing meals. Many Mauians were patients at "Kula San" in the years before TB was brought under control. *Kula Hospital*

70 **Kula Hospital**

More than 500 guests attend a lūʻau celebrating the opening of Kula General Hospital on the grounds of the sanitarium in August 1932. Tables were set up on the tennis court outside the new building. In 1937 a new five-story sanitarium building—boasting Maui's first passenger elevators—was erected next to the one-story 1932 structure. The sanitarium maintained its own dairy and farm and continued to care for tuberculosis patients until the 1960s, when its focus shifted to chronic disease and long-term care. The one-story building is still in use as a clinic.

St. John's Episcopal Church

70 **Eddie Tam's Jazz Orchestra**

Eddie Tam is best remembered as the politician who was given the honorary title of "mayor" when he was chairman of the Board of Supervisors from 1948 to 1966. But Eddie actually began his career by managing entertainers. Here he poses with his Jazz Orchestra in 1923 at the Kula Sanitarium tennis court. Eddie squats, hat in hand, while the musicians at left are Arthur Enos, Eddie Kenolio, Frank Kenolio, Arthur Keanini, Edmund Enos and Robert Makaiwi.

Stephanie Ohigashi Collection

71 **Sun Mei Ranch**

Sun Mei, the brother of Dr. Sun Yat-Sen, owned a 3,000-acre ranch in Kamaʻole, near Kēōkea. Sun Yat-Sen himself spent several years in Kula, moving his family there for their safety during the height of his revolutionary organization work in China. Many of the Chinese in Kula helped support Sun Yat-Sen's efforts, and they celebrated with a parade in 1911 when he successfully overthrew the Manchu Empire and became the first president of the Republic of China. A park near the site of his brother's ranch is dedicated to Sun Yat-Sen. *St. John's Episcopal Church*

Cattle Drive at ʻUlupalakua

The trek to Waiopai, on the opposite side of the mountain, was about 50 miles and took two days. The four or five hundred head of cattle to be fattened there annually were prized stock and had to be moved with care. The first night's stop was always at Ulupalakua Ranch. It was the most talked about place on Maui and had a history which read like a Greek tragedy set in tropical latitudes. In the Polynesian language the name had enormous significance; Ulupalakua means Ripe Breadfruit of the Gods, and it was so-called because wealth and profusion bordering on the supernatural were in the district. Its lush acres lay in a protective pocket which the gusty Trade-winds, which blow for nine months of the year in Hawaii, never reached…

About three o'clock we entered a long avenue of eucalyptus and Pride of India trees. The slowly moving herd of steers raised a cloud of golden dust with their feet and off in the southwest red Kahoolawe lay in the path of the falling sun. Half an hour's ride brought us to majestic gardens. A long concrete walk led back to a many-winged house sitting under towering camphor, breadfruit, and kukui trees.

Ulupalakua paniolos coming in from work greeted our men delightedly, and opened gates into a green pasture where the tired cattle could graze and drink their fill before going on the next morning… My eyes drank in the loveliness of the gardens. Great urns filled with fantastic Century plants were set here and there against the trees. Violets, forget-me-nots, and pansies crowded against concrete walks and great reservoirs. The air was heavy and sweet with the smell of Easter lilies, gardenias, orange trees in bloom, and plumerias. Wild peacocks shrieked in tree-massed slopes that marched up Haleakala. The old house in its stately setting of pools and walks seemed to thrust back against the mountain as if trying to get a longer perspective on everything before it.

— *from* Born in Paradise *by Armine von Tempski*

Rose Ranch

In 1856 James Makee—a former whaling captain and successful Honolulu businessman—bought a struggling ranch founded in 1845 by Linton L. Torbert and transformed it into his Rose Ranch. Makee spent $1 million over ten years building a new house, a sugar mill, a church and a mausoleum. He and his wife, Catherine, are shown here with ranch visitors *(standing at back)* and five of their eight children *(seated in the foreground)*. Now known as 'Ulupalakua Ranch, it comprises 20,000 acres, including 23 acres of vineyards, and is owned by the Erdman family.

'Ulupalakua Ranch

Rose Ranch House
The Makees' home was famous for gracious living. Eight detached buildings surrounded large living quarters for the family. Catherine Makee created luxurious flower beds, while concrete paths channeled rain into cisterns. The original main house, pictured here, was destroyed by fire in 1976, but a cottage built for visits by Hawai'i's King Kalākaua still stands and has been renovated as a tasting room for wines produced on the ranch by Tedeschi Vineyards. One room in the cottage displays photos and mementos of the ranch's rich history. *'Ulupalakua Ranch*

73 ‘Ulupalakua Mill

After Capt. James Makee purchased the struggling ‘Ulupalakua plantation, he planted thousands of trees, imported cattle and built this sugar mill to process the cane he grew. At its peak in the 1860s, the plantation was one of the largest in the Islands. Here the mill and a nearby house are pictured ca. 1880. Remnants of the mill's chimneys can still be seen today in the pasture behind ‘Ulupalakua Ranch's headquarters and store. *Hawai'i State Archives*

"A man is crippled only if he believes so in his mind."

Papa had been out hunting pheasants one day in 1910 when the accident happened. He had dismounted to cinch up his saddle, and rested his shotgun, barrel up, against a tree. At the moment he mounted and reached for the shotgun, the horse bolted, causing the hair trigger to go off. It sent a full load of buckshot into Papa's left hand and embedded 69 pellets in his side.

Determined not to lose consciousness, he wrapped his badly bleeding hand in his neckerchief, and rode the six miles home to the ranch at Ulupalakua. Near collapse, he crawled to the crank phone and called his best friend, Louis Von Tempsky. Louis, or Von, as everybody called him, answered at his home miles away at Haleakala Ranch in Makawao, and he nearly foundered his best cow pony getting to Ulupalakua. He arrived before Dr. Osmers could get there from Wailuku in his car, and found Papa on the bed, unconscious from loss of blood. Papa woke to find Von trying to make him swallow eggnog spiked with whiskey.

When the doctor arrived, they toted Papa off to the hospital in Wailuku, where they amputated his hand between the elbow and the wrist.

While he was there, Dr. J.H. Raymond, who owned the ranch, and who had hired Papa as manager in 1908, came to the hospital. He said Papa was no longer manager, because a *mu'umu'u*, a man having only one arm, could not manage the ranch. That blow left Papa feeling like a lost soul, a deserted cripple and a useless man.

Then Mr. Henry P. Baldwin came to see him. He'd never met Papa before, but he had lost his own right arm in a mill accident.

Mr. Baldwin told Papa he knew how he was feeling, but he added that "a man is crippled only if he believes so in his mind." After Papa got out of the hospital, Mr. Baldwin gave him a job as luna at the Puunene Mill of his Hawaiian Commercial & Sugar Co.

From the first meeting with a man who had never allowed despair or fear to slow him down or defeat him, Papa said, he had learned something more about how to face life, and how to live aloha.

— Memoirs, Inez MacPhee Ashdown, 1899–1992

Hawaiian Cowboys

'Ulupalakua *paniolo* trained by champion roper and Raymond Ranch manager Angus MacPhee had to be able to handle cattle both on land and in the ocean. When MacPhee came to 'Ulupalakua in 1908, he and his *paniolo* began to clear the uplands of wild cattle. They would drive the cattle into the sea at Mākena, tie them to a boat and haul them to a ship lying offshore. The cattle were secured by a sling and hoisted aboard the ship, which then took them to the slaughterhouse in Honolulu. Raymond Ranch is now 'Ulupalakua Ranch. *'Ulupalakua Ranch*

72 'Ulupalakua Ranch Office

Folklore has it that this little building was used as a jail by Capt. James Makee for lazy Rose Ranch employees who refused to work—but current 'Ulupalakua Ranch owner C. Pardee Erdman says the building was simply an office. Now providing storage for Tedeschi Vineyards, the building was formerly the winery's public tasting room. Visitors now taste Tedeschi's grape and pineapple wines in a restored guest cottage said to have been visited by King Kalākaua, located just across the lawn from this building. *Maui Historical Society*

Resources

Bartholomew, Gail (ed.), *The Index to The Maui News*, 1900–1932, Wailuku: Maui Historical Society, 1985.

Bartholomew, Gail (ed.), *The Index to The Maui News*, 1933–1950, Wailuku: Maui Historical Society, 1991.

Bartholomew, Gail, and Bren Bailey, *Maui Remembers—A Local History*, Honolulu: Mutual Publishing, 1994.

Duensing, Dawn E. (ed.), *Pa'ia: Evolution of a Community*, Pā'ia: Pa'ia Main Street Association, 1998.

Ethnic Studies Oral History Project, Stores and Storekeepers of Paia and Puunene, Maui, Honolulu: University of Hawai'i-Mānoa, 1980.

Haleakala Ranch, One Hundredth Anniversary, Wailuku: *The Maui News*, 1989.

Kahului Railroad Stories, Kahului: First Light Studios, 2000.

Mark, Diane Mei Lin, *Seasons of Light: The History of Chinese Christian Churches in Hawaii*, Honolulu: Chinese Christian Association of Hawaii, 1989.

Mark, Diane Mei Lin, *The Chinese in Kula*, Honolulu: Hawaii Chinese History Center, 1975.

Paia Main Street Association, *Paia Historic Building Guide and Walking Tour*, Pā'ia: Pa'ia Main Street Association, 1995.

Rho, Marguerite, and Charles Regal, *Alexander & Baldwin: Ninety Years a Corporation, 1900–1990*, Honolulu: Ampersand, 1990.

Stone, Scott C., *St. Joseph Church 1911–1997*, Makawao: St. Joseph Church, 1997.

Tabrah, Ruth M., and Joan Fukumoto, *A Grateful Past, A Promising Future: The First Years of Honpa Hongwanji in Hawaii, 1889–1989*, Honolulu: Hongpa Hongwanji Mission of Hawaii, 1989.

The Bank of Maui, Ltd., Wailuku: Bank of Maui, 1919.

The Maui News, Wailuku: Maui Publishing Co.

Tysseland, Elsie, *St. John's Episcopal Church, 1900–2000*, Kēōkea: St. John's Episcopal Church, 2000.

Ueoka, Noriyuki and Judy Matoi, *Ninetieth Anniversary: Mantokuji Mission of Paia*, Maui, Paia Mantokuji Mission, 1996.

Von Tempski, Armine, *Born in Paradise*, Woodbridge, Conn., Ox Bow Press, 1995.

Index

	MAP	PAGE
Bank of Hawaii, Ha'iku	34	50
Bank of Hawaii, Pa'ia	18	27
Camp Maui	36	51
Club Rodeo	44	67
Crook Camp	47	73
Crossroads Service	45	68, 69, 70
Dang Dry Goods	7	7
Emil Balthazar Bridge	50	71
First Hawaiian Bank	22	33
Fong Store	69	108, 109
Fred Baldwin Memorial Home	39	57
Haiku Fruit & Packing Co.	35	47
Haiku House	33	49
Haleakala Church	67	103
Haleakala Polo Field	54	78
Haleakala Ranch	53	79, 80, 81
Haleakala Ranch HQ	52	77
Haliimaile Plantation	57	89
Haliimaile Store	56	88
Hardy House	51	74
Haserot Cannery	32	46
Hew Store	3	11
Holomua Road	28	40
Holy Ghost Church	61	98–99
Holy Rosary Church	25	37

	MAP	PAGE
Ikeda Store	17	25
Kaluanui	41	60, 61, 62, 63
Kaonoulu Ranch	63	92, 93
Keāhua Village	55	82, 84, 85, 86, 87
Keokea School	66	107
Kitada Kau Kau Korner	42	64
Komoda Store	43	65
Kuiaha Gulch	31	45
Kula Botanical Garden	62	90
Kula Extension Service	60	96, 97
Kula Hospital	70	111
Kula Sanitarium	70	110, 111, 112
Kwock Hing Society	68	105
Liberty Cafe	11	14
Lower Paia Theatre	4	8, 9, 10
Makawao Post Office	46	71
Makawao Union Church	37	54, 55
Matsui Restaurant	6	7
Maui Agricultural Co.	21	32
Maui Country Club	1	19
Maui High School	29	42, 43
Maunaolu Community College	40	58, 59
Morihara Store	59	95
N. Kobayashi Auto Supply	13	22, 23

	MAP	PAGE
Nagata Store	5	7
Oskie Rice Pasture	48	52
Paia Clothes Cleaners	16	24
Paia Community House	38	56
Pā'ia Fire Site	10	13
Paia Hongwanji Mission	24	36
Paia Hospital	27	39
Paia Mantokuji Mission	15	16, 17
Paia Mercantile	12	15
Paia Mill	20	31
Paia Railroad Depot	19	28, 29, 30
Paia School	26	38
Paia Store	23	34, 35
Pā'ia USO	14	21
Pauwela Store	30	44
Pulehu Chapel	58	94
St. John's Episcopal Church	65	100, 102
St. Joseph Church	49	75
Sun Mei Ranch	71	113
Tavares Bay	2	18
'Ulupalakua Mill	73	117
'Ulupalakua Ranch	72	120
Waiohuli Pen	64	92
Wimpy's Corner	9	7
Wong Store	8	7

122